La Cage aux folles

VOCAL selections

THE BROADWAY MUSICAL COMEDY

Music and Lyrics by
JERRY HERMAN
Arranged by
PATRICK HOLLAND

3 We Are What We Are
6 A Little More Mascara
12 With You On My Arm
15 Song On The Sand
20 La Cage Aux Folles
33 I Am What I Am
38 Masculinity
42 Look Over There
49 The Best Of Times

HAL LEONARD PUBLISHING CORPORATION

Home Office:
960 East Mark Street
Winona MN 55987

National Sales Office:
8112 West Bluemound Road
Milwaukee WI 53213

© 1983 La Cage Co.

Rehearsal

WE ARE WHAT WE ARE

From the Broadway musical "La Cage Aux Folles"

Music and Lyric by
JERRY HERMAN

Lively

We are what we are, and what we are is an il - lu - sion.
We are what we are, half a bras - siere, is half a sus - pen - der;

We love how it feels put - ting on heels caus - ing con - fu - sion. We
half real and half fluff, you'll find it tough guess - ing our gen - der. So

face life tho' it's some - times sweet and some - times bit - ter, face life with a
just (whistle) if we please you that's the way to show us, just (whistle) 'cause you'll

© 1983 JERRY HERMAN
All rights Controlled by JERRYCO MUSIC CO.
Exclusive Agent: EDWIN H. MORRIS & COMPANY, A Division of MPL Communications, Inc.
International Copyright Secured   Made in U.S.A.   All Rights Reserved

lit - tle guts and lots of glit - ter. Look un - der our frocks, gir - dles and
love us once you get to know us. Look un - der our glitz, mus - cles and

jocks, prov - ing we are what ___ we are. ___
tits, prov - ing we are what ___ we

are. ___

We face life tho' its some-times sweet and some-times bit - ter, face life with a lit - tle guts and lots of glit - ter. Look un - der our frocks gir - dles and jocks, prov - ing we are what _____ we are.

A LITTLE MORE MASCARA

From the Broadway musical "La Cage Aux Folles"

Music and Lyric by
JERRY HERMAN

Freely

Once a-gain, I'm a lit-tle de-pressed by the tired old face that I see; Once a-gain, it is time to be some-one, who's an-y-one oth-er than me. With a rare com-bi-na-tion of girl-ish ex-cite-ment and man-ly re-straint, I po-

si - tion my pre-cious as - sort-ment of pow - ders and pen - cils and paint, So when

ev - er I feel that my place in this world is be - gin-ning to crash, I ap -

ply one great stroke of mas - ca - ra to my ra - ther limp up - per lash, and I can

cope a - gain, Good God! there's hope a - gain. When life _____ is a real
I _____ count my crow's

bitch a - gain _____ and my old sense of hu - mor has up and gone, _____
feet a - gain _____ and tire of this per - pet - u - al mar - a - thon, _____

It's time _____ for the big switch a - gain; _____
I put _____ down the big john seat a - gain, _____

I put a lit - tle more mas - ca - ra on. _____ When
And put a lit - tle more mas - ca - ra

And ev - 'ry - thing's spar - kle dust, bu - gle beads,
on. an - kle straps, mar - i - bu,

os - trich plumes, / shal - i - mar!

When it's a bead - ed lash that you look _ / It's worth suck - ing in my gut and gird' - ling _ my

through; _____ 'cause when I feel glam - or - ous, el - e - gant, / rear; _____ 'cause ev' - ry - thing's rav - ish - ing, sen - su - al,

beau - ti - ful, the world _ that I'm look - ing at's beau - ti - ful _ / fab - u - lous, when Al - bin is tucked a - way and Za - Za is

too! / here!

When my _ lit - tle road _____ has a few bumps a - gain, _____ / When ev - ry - thing slides _____ down the old tubes a - gain, _____

Guitar Tacet

and I need some-thing le-vel to lean up on, ____
and my old self es-teem has be-gun to drift, ____

put on my sling pumps a-gain, ____ and wham! this ug-ly
strap on my fake boobs a-gain, ____ and lit-er-al-ly

duck-ling is a swan! ____ So when my spir-it starts to sag ____ I
give my-self a lift! ____ So when it's cold and when it's bleak ____ I

hus-tle out my high-est drag ____ and put a lit-tle more mas-ca-ra
sim-ply rouge the oth-er cheek, ____ and for

Lyrics (vocal line):

on! _____ And ev'-ry-thing's I can face an-oth-er day__ in

slip-per sat-in lin-ge-rie,__ To make de-press-ion dis-ap-pear__ I

screw some rhine-stones on my ear__ and put my broach-es and ti-a-ra and a lit-tle

more mas-ca-ra on! _____

Chord symbols: Gmaj9, D7 (Guitar Tacet), Am(add9), D7(#9), D7, Am(add9), D7(#9), D7, Am9, Am7, D7, Am9, D7(#9), D7, Am(add9), D7(#9), D7, Am(add9), D7(#9), D, Gmaj9

WITH YOU ON MY ARM

From the Broadway musical "La Cage Aux Folles"

Music and Lyric by
JERRY HERMAN

Life is a cel-e-bra-tion with you on my arm. Walk-ing's a new sen-sa-tion with you on my arm. Each time I

© 1983 JERRY HERMAN
All rights Controlled by JERRYCO MUSIC CO.
Exclusive Agent: EDWIN H. MORRIS & COMPANY, A Division of MPL Communications, Inc.
International Copyright Secured   Made in U.S.A.   All Rights Reserved

face a morn-ing that's bor-ing and bland, with you __ it looks

good, with you __ it looks great, with you __ it looks grand! _____

Some-how you've put a per-ma-nent

star in my eye. E-ven the

SONG ON THE SAND
(LA DA DA DA)
From the Broadway musical "La Cage Aux Folles"

Music and Lyric by
JERRY HERMAN

Wistfully

Do you re-call that wind-y lit-tle beach we walked a-long? That af-ter-noon in fall, that af-ter-noon we met? A fel-la with a con-cer-ti-na sang; what was the song? It's strange what we re-call, and

© 1983 JERRY HERMAN
All Rights Controlled by JERRYCO MUSIC CO.
Exclusive Agent: EDWIN H. MORRIS & COMPANY, A Division of MPL Communications, Inc.
International Copyright Secured   Made in U.S.A.   All Rights Reserved

odd what we for-get. I heard la __ da da da __ da da da __ as we walked on the sand. I heard

la __ da da da, __ I be-lieve __ it was ear-ly Sep-tem-ber. Through the

crash __ of the waves __ I could tell __ that the words __ were ro-man-tic; some-thing a-bout

shar-ing, some-thing a-bout al-ways. Tho' the years __ race a-long, __ I still

think ___ of our song ___ on the sand and I still ___ try and search ___ for the words ___ I can bare-ly re-mem-ber. Tho' the time ___ tum-bles by, ___ there is one ___ thing that I ___ am for-ev-er cer-tain of: I hear la ___ da da da ___ da da da ___ da da da ___ da da da, and I'm young and in love.

I be - lieve __ it was ear - ly Sep - tem - ber. Through the crash __ of the waves __ I could tell __ that the words __ were ro - man - tic; some -thing a -bout shar -ing, some -thing a -bout al -ways. Tho' the years __ race a -long, __ I still think __ of our song __ on the sand and I

still ___ try and search ___ for the words ___ I can bare -ly re - mem - ber. Tho' the

time ___ tum -bles by, ___ there is one ___ thing that I ___ am for - ev - er cer - tain

of: I hear la ___ da da da ___ da da da ___ da da da da da

da, and I'm young and in love. ___

LA CAGE AUX FOLLES
From the Broadway musical "La Cage Aux Folles"

Music and Lyric by
JERRY HERMAN

It's rath-er gaud-y but it's al-so rath-er grand, and while the wait-er pads your check, he'll kiss your hand. The clev-er gi-go-los ro-mance the wealth-y ma-trons at La

It's slight-ly "for-ties" and a lit-tle bit "New Wave," you may be danc-ing with a girl who needs a shave, Where both the riff-raff and the roy-al-ty are pa-trons at La

Cage Aux Folles._____ Cage Aux Folles._____ La Cage Aux Folles,_____

_____ the mai-tre-d' is dash-ing, Cage Aux Folles,_____ the hat-check

girl is flash-ing We im-port the drinks that you buy,_____ (So the

Per - ri - er is Can - a - da Dry!)___ Ec - cen - tric

coup - les al - ways punc - tu - ate the scene;_____ A pair of eu - nuchs and a

nun with a Ma - rine To feel a - live you get a lim - o - sine to

drive you to La Cage Aux Folles.___

It's bad and beau-ti-ful, it's
Go for the mys-ter-y, the

bawd-y, and bi-zarre,
mag-ic, and the mood,

I know a duch-ess who got preg-nant at the
A-void the hus-tlers, and the men's-room, and the

bar.
food.

Just who is who, and what is what, is quite the ques-tion at La
For you get glam-our and ro-mance, and in-di-ges-tion at La

Guitar Tacet

Cage Aux Folles.

Cage Aux

Folles. _____ La Cage Aux Folles _____ a St. Tro-

pex tra-di-tion, Cage Aux Folles _____ you'll lose each in-hi-bi-tion,

All week long we're won-der-ing who _____ left a green gi-ven-chy

gown in the loo. _____ You go a-lone to have the eve'-ning of your

life, you meet your mis-tress, and your boy-friend, and your wife.

It's a bo-nan-za, it's a mad ex-tra-va-gan-za, at La Cage Aux Folles.

You cross the thresh-old, and your brid-ges have been burned, the bar is cheer-ing, for the

Guitar Tacet

duch - ess has re - turned. The mood's con - ta - gious, you can bring your whole out -

Accel. poco a poco

ra - geous en - tou - rage.

a tempo

It's so e - clec - tic, ef - fer - ves - cent, and e - lec - tric, at La Cage

piv f

Aux Folles.

faster to end

cres - cen - do

I AM WHAT I AM
From the Broadway musical "La Cage Aux Folles"

Music and Lyric by
JERRY HERMAN

love each feath-er and each span-gle, why not__ try and see things from a diff'-rent an-gle?
you don't like the style I bring it My song,__ so at least re-spect my right to sing it,

Your life__ is a sham, 'til__ you can shout out__ loud, "I am what I

Twice as Fast

am."_____ I am_____ what I

am and_____ what I am needs_____ no ex-

cus - es. I deal my own

deck some - times the ace, some - times, the

deuc - es.
There's one life, and there's
It's one high time that I

no re - turn and no de - pos - it; one life,
blow my horn and sound my trump - et, High time,

MASCULINITY

From the Broadway musical "La Cage Aux Folles"

Music and Lyric by
JERRY HERMAN

Think of this as mas-cu-line toast, and mas-cu-line but-ter, grunt like an ape, and growl like a ti-ger, read-y for spread-ing by a mas-cu-line hand. give us a roar-ing snor-ing mas-cu-line laugh: (Ha!) Pick up that Try and re-

Cm7-5   B♭maj7   F7   Gm(add 9)   Guitar Tacet

knife and make be - lieve it's a ma - che - te,   it - 'll take
mem - ber that John Wayne was not so - pra - no,   try keep - ing it

Gm9   C9/G   Cm/E♭   Ddim   Cm7   F7

all your strength and stead - y nerves for hack - ing your way thru the cher - ry pre - serves.
gruff and ruff and low, (Ha! Ha!) Try more of John Wayne and less Brid - get Bar - dot.

rit.

B♭   Gm   Cm7   F6   Cm7   F7

Think of John Wayne and Jean - Paul Bel - mon - do, _____
Think of De - Gaulle, and think of Ras - pu - tin, _____

a tempo

Gm   Fm6   G7   Guitar Tacet

Think of the Le - gion - aires and Char - le - magne's men.   So like a
Think like a Dan - iel march - ing in - to the den.   While try - ing to

ste - ve - dore you grab your cup, and if (God for - bid!) that your pink - y pops up! You can
join the burl - y brutes if you for - get that your ny - lons are un - der your boots, you can

climb back up the moun - tain once a - gain.
climb back up the moun - tain once a -

Think of these as gain.

Think Ghen - gis Kahn and think Ta - ras Bul - ba.

Think of At - til - la's huns, and Ro - bin - hood's men. And try not to weak - en or col - lapse if they dis - cov - er the pet - ti - coat un - der your chaps, you can climb back up the moun - tain once _____ a - gain. _____

first tempo

Guitar Tacet

LOOK OVER THERE
From the Broadway musical "La Cage Aux Folles"

Music and Lyric by
JERRY HERMAN

Not too slowly (in 1)

How of-ten is some-one con-cerned with the ti-ni-est thread of your life?

Con-cerned with what-ev-er you feel, and what-

© 1983 JERRY HERMAN
All rights Controlled by JERRYCO MUSIC CO.
Exclusive Agent: EDWIN H. MORRIS & COMPANY, A Division of MPL Communications, Inc.
International Copyright Secured   Made in U.S.A.   All Rights Reserved

ev - er you touch? _____ Look o - ver there, _____ Look o - ver there; _____ Some - bod - y cares _____ that _____ much. _____ How of - ten does some - bod - y sense that you

need them with - out be - ing told? When you have a

hurt in your heart you're too proud to dis - close? _____

Look o - ver there, _____ Look o - ver there; _____

_____ Some - bod - y al - ways _____

So count all the loves who will love you from now 'til the end of your life. And when you have add - ed the loves who have loved you be - fore, Look o - ver there;

Look o - ver there; _____ Some - bod - y

loves _____ you _____ more. _____

When your world spins too more. _____

Recording Session

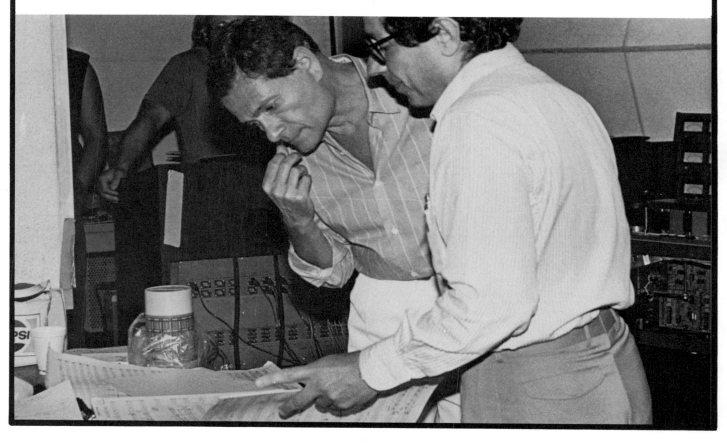

THE BEST OF TIMES

From the Broadway musical "La Cage Aux Folles"

Music and Lyric by
JERRY HERMAN

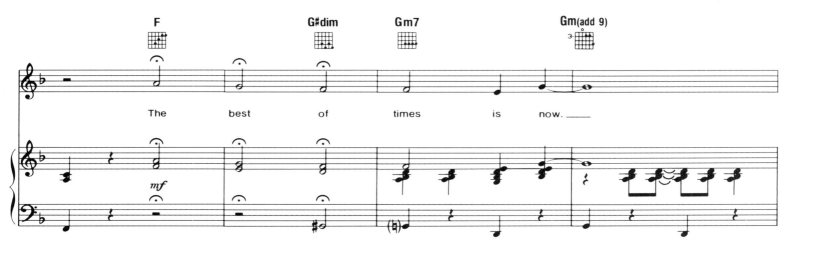

The best of times is now. ____

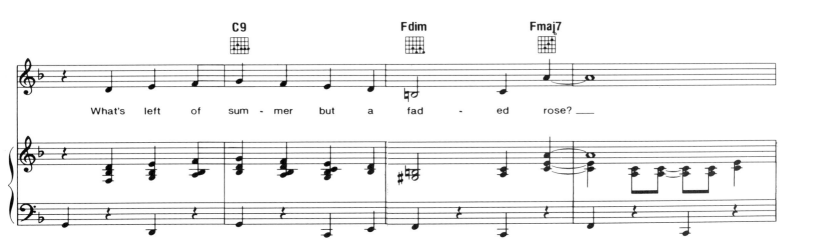

What's left of sum - mer but a fad - ed rose? ____

© 1983 JERRY HERMAN
All rights Controlled by JERRYCO MUSIC CO.
Exclusive Agent: EDWIN H. MORRIS & COMPANY, A Division of MPL Communications, Inc.
International Copyright Secured   Made in U.S.A   All Rights Reserved

The best of times is now.

As for to - mor - row, well, who knows? Who knows? Who

knows? So hold this mo - ment fast

and live and love as hard as you know how.

And make this mo-ment last be-cause the best of times is now, is now, is now. Now, not some for-got-ten yes-ter-day.

Now, to-mor-row is too far a-way.

So hold this mo-ment fast,

and live and love as hard as you know how.

And make this mo - ment last

be - cause the best of times is now, is now, is

now. The best of

times is now. What's left of sum - mer but a

molto ritard.

Slower

fad - ed rose? ____ The best of

times is now. ____ As for to - mor - row, well, who

knows? Who knows? Who knows? So hold this

mo - ment fast ____ and live and love as hard as

Jerry Herman